D1528063

A New Dad's Pocket Book of Bad Dad Jokes!

This book belongs to the Dad of...

For new Dads, old Dads, could be, would be and should be Dads this book is your ticket to the Dad Joke Hall of Fame! Get ready for eye-rolling puns and cringeworthy jokes for all occasions that will have everyone in the your extended family groaning in unison. We're here to load your comedy cannon with pun-tastic ammunition and witty quips that'll leave anyone who dares to listen in splits, or at the very least in stitches!

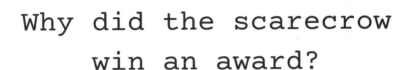

Why did the scarecrow win an award?

Because he was outstanding in his field!

How do you organise a party in outer space?

You Planet!

Why did Mickey mouse go to outer space?

To find Pluto!

Did you hear about the
kidnapping out at the
playground?

They woke up!

Z Z Z

Why don't skeletons
fight each other

They don't have the
guts to do it!

Why did the bicycle
fall over?

Because it was two
tyred!

What do you call a fish
with no eyes?

Fsh

Why did the fisherman
suddenly change
direction of his boat?

Just for the halibut.

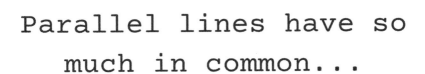

Parallel lines have so
much in common...

It's such a shame they
will never meet.

What do you call cheese that's not yours?

Nacho cheese!

What do you call a dinosaur made of cheese?

Gorgonzilla!

Why don't scientists
trust atoms?

Because they make up
everything.

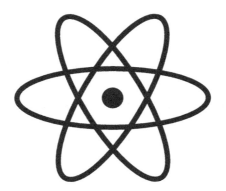

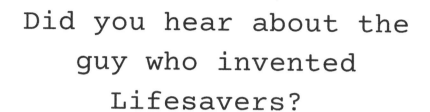

Did you hear about the guy who invented Lifesavers?

He made a mint!

What do you call a train loaded with bubble gum?

A chew-chew train!

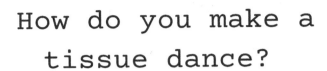

How do you make a
tissue dance?

You put a little boogie
in it.

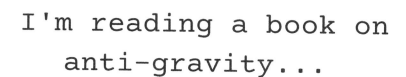

I'm reading a book on anti-gravity...

It's impossible to put down!

What kinds of books do planets usually like to read?

Comet books!

How do you catch a squirrel?

Climb a tree and act like a nut!

I'm on a seafood diet.

I see food, and I eat it!

What did the baby corn say to its mom?

Where's my pop-corn?

What do you call a
bear with no teeth?

A gummy bear.

Did you hear about the cheese factory explosion?

There was nothing left but de-brie.

How does a penguin
build its house?

Igloos it together!

Where does a snowman
get the weather report?

The winternet!

What's orange and
sounds like a parrot?

A carrot!

When potatoes have
babies, what are they
called?

Tater tots.

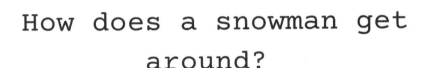

How does a snowman get around?

By riding an icicle!

What did the tree say after a long, cold winter?

What a re-leaf!

I used to be a baker...

...but I couldn't make enough dough

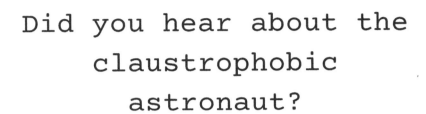

Did you hear about the claustrophobic astronaut?

He just needed a little space.

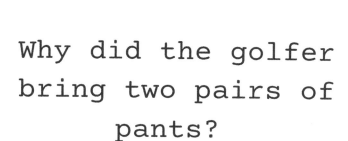

Why did the golfer
bring two pairs of
pants?

In case he got a hole
in one.

What did one wall say
to the other wall?

"I'll meet you at the
corner!"

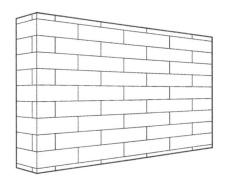

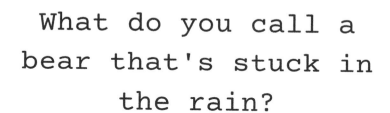

What do you call a
bear that's stuck in
the rain?

A drizzly bear.

I thought there was
only 25 letters in the
alphabet...

...I don't know Y.

How do you make holy water?

You boil the hell out of it.

I couldn't figure out
how to put my seatbelt
on...

...Then it clicked!

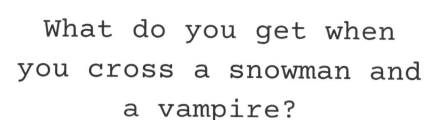

What do you get when
you cross a snowman and
a vampire?

Frostbite!

What's in a ghost's
nose?

BOOOOOgers!

What do you call a
dinosaur with an
extensive vocabulary?

A thesaurus!

Why can't you hear a pterodactyl go to the bathroom?

Because the "P" is silent!

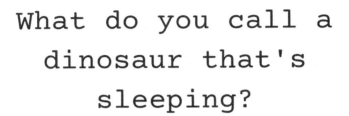

What do you call a
dinosaur that's
sleeping?

A dino-snore!

How do you know if there's a dinosaur in your refrigerator?

The door won't close!

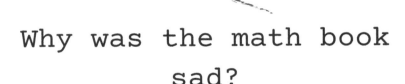

Why was the math book sad?

Because it had too many problems!

What did one ion say to its friend?

I've got my ion you.

How do you fix a broken tuba?

With a tuba glue!

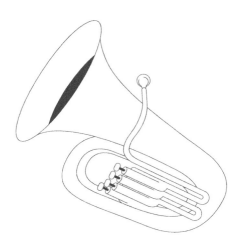

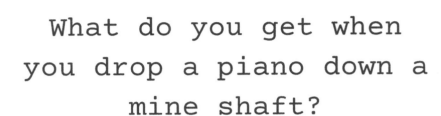

What do you get when you drop a piano down a mine shaft?

A flat minor.

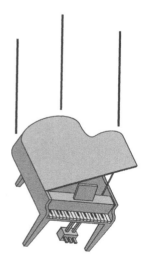

Why did the astronaut
break up with his
girlfriend?

He needed space.

What did Mars say to Saturn?

"Give me a ring sometime!"

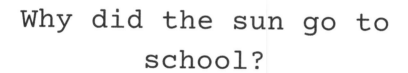

Why did the sun go to school?

To get a little brighter.

My friend is obsessed with the moon...

..I'm hoping it's just a phase.

What do you do when you throw a space party?

You "meteor" guests!

Why are fish so smart?

Because the live in schools!

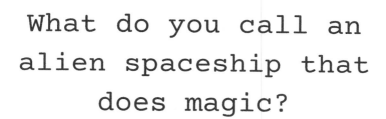

What do you call an alien spaceship that does magic?

A flying saucer-er!

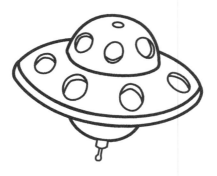

Did you hear about the astronaut who stepped on chewing gum?

He got stuck in orbit!

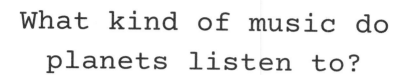

What kind of music do planets listen to?

Neptunes!

Why did the tomato turn red?

Because it saw the salad dressing!

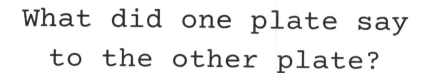

What did one plate say
to the other plate?

"Lunch is on me!"

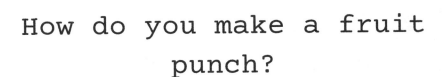

How do you make a fruit
punch?

Give it boxing lessons!

What did the mayonnaise say to the refrigerator?

"Close the door, I'm dressing!"

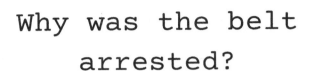

Why was the belt
arrested?

Because it was holding
up a pair of pants!

Why did the dough go to therapy?

Because it kneaded some emotional support!

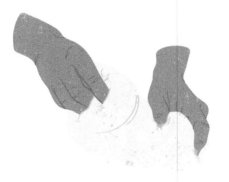

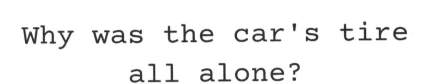

Why was the car's tire
all alone?

Because it had lost all
its "wheel" friends!

What do you call a car that's been left out in the sun too long?

A "hot rod"!

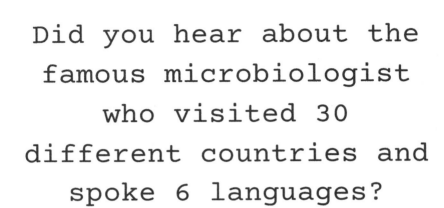

Did you hear about the famous microbiologist who visited 30 different countries and spoke 6 languages?

He was a man of many cultures.

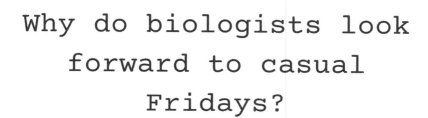

Why do biologists look forward to casual Fridays?

They're allowed to wear genes to work.

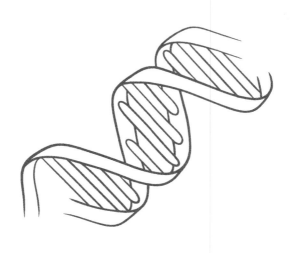

A neutron walked into a bar and asked the bartender, "How much is a drink?"

The bartender replied, "For you, no charge."

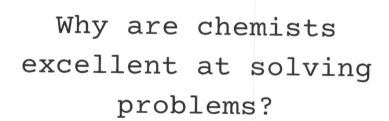

Why are chemists
excellent at solving
problems?

They have all the
solutions!

The earth's rotation
really makes my day.

Two hydrogen atoms meet. One says, "I've lost my electron." The other says, "Are you sure?" The first replies, "Yes, I'm positive!"

What's E.T. short for? He has little legs.

Why did the student bring a ladder to school?

Because he thought it was high school!

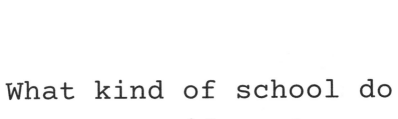

What kind of school do you go to if you're an ice cream lover?

Sundae school!

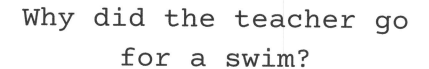

Why did the teacher go
for a swim?

To test the waters!

What is a snakes
favourite school
subject?

Hissssssssstory!

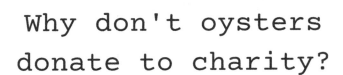

Why don't oysters
donate to charity?

Because they are
shellfish!

Did you hear about the
red and blue ships that
collided?

All the sailors were
marooned.

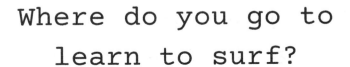

Where do you go to
learn to surf?

A boarding school.

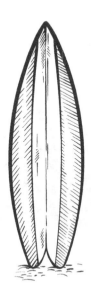

A duck walks into a bar and buys everyone a round.

He tells the bartender, "Put it on my bill."

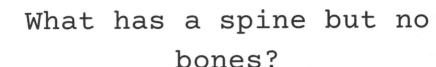

What has a spine but no bones?

A book.

Why did the teacher where sunglasses in the classroom?

Because her students were so bright!

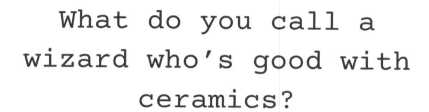

What do you call a wizard who's good with ceramics?

Harry Pottery.

How did Vikings
communicate over long
distances?

By Norse code!

Why don't the other
animals like playing
basketball with pigs?

They're ball hogs!

My boss told me to
have a good day...

...So I didn't go into
work.

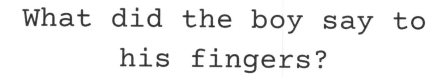

What did the boy say to his fingers?

I'm counting on you.

Why are balloons so expensive?

Inflation!

What kind of music do Santa's elves listen to?

Wrap music.

When does Friday come before Thursday?

In the dictionary.

What did the tree say when spring finally arrived?

What a re-leaf.

Did you hear about the guy who was afraid of hurdles?

He got over it.

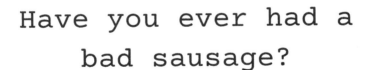

Have you ever had a
bad sausage?

It's the wurst.

How do you make an
apple turnover?

Push it down a hill.

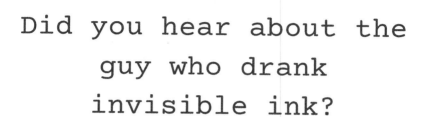

Did you hear about the guy who drank invisible ink?

He's still at the hospital waiting to be seen.

Did you hear about the
cat that ate a lemon?

Now it's a sour puss.

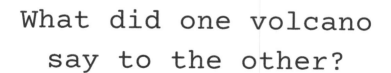

What did one volcano
say to the other?

I lava you!

What do lawyers wear
to work?

Law suits!

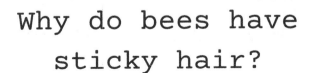

Why do bees have
sticky hair?

Because they use a
honeycomb!

What is the best way
to cook an alligator?

In a croc-pot!

What do you call a can opener that doesn't work?

A can't opener!

Did you hear about the guys selling a broken guitar?

No strings attached!

Have you read the book about super glue?

It's really hard to put down!

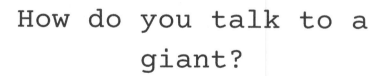

How do you talk to a giant?

Use really big words!

What did the hat say to the scarf?

You hang around while I go on ahead.

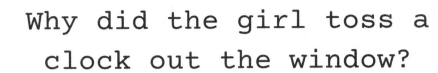

Why did the girl toss a clock out the window?

She wanted to see time fly.

Why was the snowman looking in the bag of carrots?

He was picking his nose.

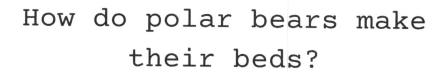

How do polar bears make their beds?

With sheets of ice and blankets of snow.

What do you get when you cross Santa Claus with a space ship?

A U-F-Ho-Ho-Ho!

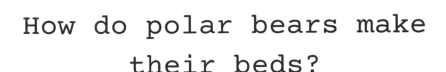

How do polar bears make their beds?

With sheets of ice and blankets of snow.

Where did the lettuce go to have a few drinks?

The salad bar.

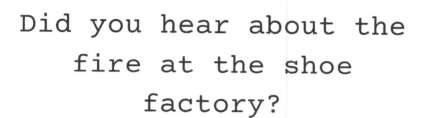

Did you hear about the fire at the shoe factory?

Sadly, many soles were lost.

What happens if a strawberry gets run over crossing the street?

It causes a traffic jam!

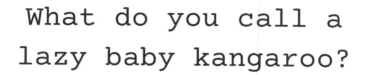

What do you call a
lazy baby kangaroo?

A pouch potato!

What did the vet say
to the cat?

How are you feline?

Did you hear about the
shark that ate a clown?

It felt funny after.

I'm so good at
sleeping...
...I can do it with my
eyes closed!

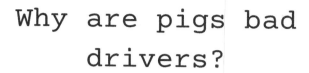

Why are pigs bad
drivers?

They hog the road.

Getting paid to sleep
would be my dream job.

Which USA state has the most streets

Rhode Island!

What's an astronaut's favorite part of a computer?

The space bar

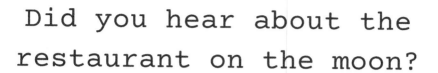

Did you hear about the restaurant on the moon?

Great food, no atmosphere.

What is the Easter bunny's favorite type of music?

Hip-hop.

A ham sandwich walks into a bar and orders a beer.

The bartender says, "Sorry, we don't serve food here."

It was my son's fourth birthday was today.

When he came to see me, I didn't recognize him at first. I had never seen him be four.

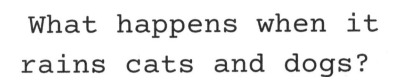

What happens when it
rains cats and dogs?

You have to be careful
not to step in a
poodle.

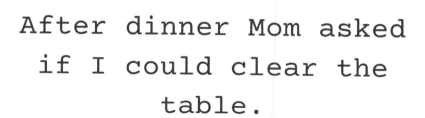

After dinner Mom asked
if I could clear the
table.

I needed a running
start, but I made it.

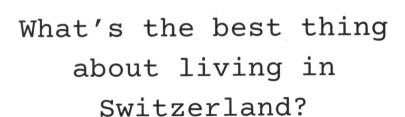

What's the best thing about living in Switzerland?

I don't know, but the flag is a big plus!

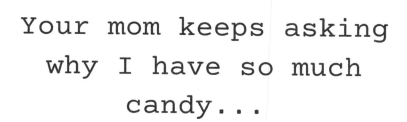

Your mom keeps asking why I have so much candy...

She doesn't know I always keep a few Twix up my sleeve.

Wanna hear one last
joke about pizza?

Never mind it's too
cheesy.

REMEMBER
YOU ARE ONE...

RAD DAD

THE BEST DAD EVER!!!

Handy Hacks
for New Dad's

Being a rookie parent is no walk in the park, more like a stroll through a burning maze filled with diaper changes and sleepless nights! But don't fret; we're here to dish out some parental wisdom seasoned with a pinch of humor to steer you on your dadventure. Just remember, you're bound to fumble along the way, and sometimes your dad jokes just won't hit the mark but that's all part of the package. You're their superhero in a dad cape, but you're also the same old you. So embrace the chaos, laugh at the baby's questionable fashion choices, and enjoy the rollercoaster ride of parenthood - even if it's more sleep-deprived than an all night streaming binge!

Master the art of Dad Jokes

Start honing your dad joke skills. The cheesier, the better! Your ability to make your baby laugh or embarrase your teenager with goofy jokes will become your new superpower. Because when life gets hard we all need a good chuckle now and then!

Embrace the Dad Bod

As a new dad, you may find it challenging to maintain your pre-baby Adonis physique. My advice is to embrace the "dad bod"! Proudly wear your love handles and extra pounds as badges of honor. After all it is the official uniform of fatherhood! Don't worry, all the parental fret and stress will help melt those pounds away in years to come!

Parental Multitasking

Master the art of multitasking like a pro. As a new parent you will learn that there simply aren't enough hours in the day to only do one thing at a time. You'll soon find yourself holding a baby in one arm, assembling a crib with the other, and balancing a bottle on your foot. It's like a circus act, but with more dirty diapers and less applause.

Dad Fashion

Say goodbye to fashionable clothes for a while and embrace the new dad uniform. Dirty shirts, Stained trousers, spit-up, and mysterious unexplained food substances are all part of the deal. I recommend you start a collection of "dad shirts" where the stains are part of their charm. th se are perfect for those moments when you need to blend in with the chaos like a spit stained chameleon.

Daddy DIY

Embrace your newfound skills as a DIY dad repair man. You'll be assembling baby gear, fixing broken toys, and crafting creative fixes to everyday parenting issues with nothing but an Allen key, a scewdriver, a tube of super glue and a roll of tape! You'll soon discover that if it can't be fixed with that tool box arsenal then it's just not worth fixing.

Made in United States
North Haven, CT
18 December 2023